A
Lecture
by
Valerio Olgiati

I will be showing you four projects: three completed buildings and one competition project. I will also show you a collection of pictures that I refer to as my iconographic autobiography. It represents an attempt to explain the personal background of my own architecture. We will now begin with the first picture, and I would be grateful if we could have the lights turned off.

We begin with a photo from an exhibition of my work at the Swiss Federal Institute of Technology (ETH) in Zurich. Here you can see a collection of white models, all of which are constructed on a scale of 1:33. There is no visible context. The buildings have been, as it were, torn out of the ground, like uprooted trees. I am showing you this picture at the beginning because I am convinced that it is possible to create architecture that is not primarily contextual. Over last twenty years the question of contextuality has become all pervasive as a kind of moral basis, which is regarded as necessarily informing every architectural project. As a result, architects now primarily approach their work in terms of a reaction to their environment. However, I believe that architecture can develop out of an idea, from a thought, and that such an idea does not in principle have to be tied to the prevailing context. Historical examples can be found in temples and churches. Even barns and stables are hardly ever contextual but are nevertheless beautiful. In most cases they are beautiful buildings—buildings that have emerged from an idea, buildings that do not exclusively react to contextual, economic, technical, and functional requirements. I am convinced that today it is still possible and indeed necessary to base designs on ideas, and to create buildings that are capable of contributing to the cultural intelligence of our time.

We come now to the first project: a museum for the Swiss National Park in Zernez. The building is constructed almost completely of concrete. Here you can see one segment, a detail of a window.

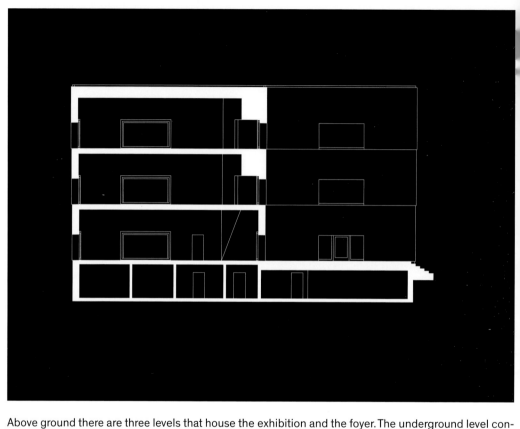

Above ground there are three levels that house the exhibition and the foyer. The underground level contains storage areas, toilets, and the building's technical facilities. In the cross section pictured here, the walls and ceilings are marked in white. The entire structure is poured in concrete and does not feature any visible details. The walls are made of insulating concrete, the ceiling of standard concrete. I am always being asked whether the building is conditioned. The answer is that there is a heating system, an air-conservation ventilation system, a lighting system, and a wireless computer system. The building could serve equally well as a contemporary art gallery. Nevertheless, none of the details are visible: the technical possibilities of the museum are not demonstrated.

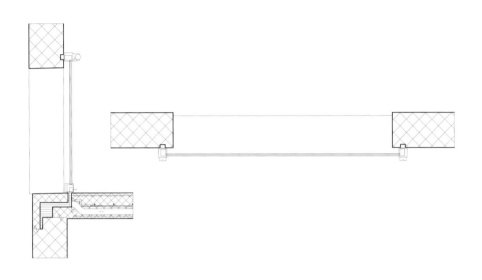

We now come to the detailed cross section and the detailed floor plan. The wall is 55 cm thick with a thermally separated casement frame of metal and glass set against it. I should point out here that in the floor plan the external side is shown facing upwards. When you look from the outside into the interior, the casement frame is not visible because it is somewhat larger than the opening in the wall. Inside the wall and beneath the frame there is a small insulated hollow space that increases the distance traveled by the cooling air across the surface and thereby reduces energy costs. The cross section of the ceiling shows the ventilation system, pre-stressing elements, computer technology, and the heating system. Not much more needs to be said about the details of the building: the entire structure has been poured in a single, monolithic layer of concrete, with no joints, or silicon.

Here you can see the components of the concrete used for the building. Usually concrete is composed of grey cement, and grey gravel sand. The gravel sand can in turn be separated into grey powdered stone, grey sand, and grey gravel. In the case of our building we have used white cement and white powdered stone. Instead of grey sand we have used small, foamed glass granules known as Liaver. Finally, we have replaced the grey gravel with Liapor, a volcanic, granular and extremely auriferous material. This mixture was used to pour the walls. The wall thickness of 55 cm allows the prevailing energy-use standards to be maintained.

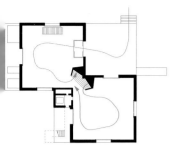 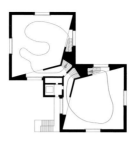 

On the upper left you can see the ground floor, in the middle the first floor and to the right the second floor. The ground plan of the building is composed of two squares, or, in three-dimensional terms, two cubes that intersect at one of their corners. This project was the winning submission in a competition. At the time we found out that we could meet all of the client's very complex requirements with six equally sized rooms. We therefore decided not to design a building made up, as it were, of different pieces of a puzzle. This would have meant dealing with constant conflicts due to missing pieces and the creation of leftover spaces that were either unusable or ugly. The basic idea was thus to create six equal, operational spaces, a sort of genetic program for the building, if you will. I want to use the following picture to take you on a tour of the building. The orange line traces the route as you ascend through the building and the green line the route as you descend. From the street you enter the building via a platform into the foyer where you find a staircase that splits as you ascend, allowing you to go right or left. When you reach the first upper level you enter the first room by one of four openings into the space. From here you leave the room via another opening and take another staircase to the second level. Here you encounter exactly the same type of space and leave it again in the same way. However, in this case you do not climb another staircase but instead walk along a corridor and enter the next exhibition room. This room is also exactly the same as the two previous ones. From here, the same system leads you down through the building until you ultimately come to the same staircase from where you began your tour. Thus, on the upper levels you encounter the same space four times, and at the ground level the same spatial system, but without dividing walls—a labyrinthine system with repetitions, and rooms equipped with windows facing in each of the cardinal directions.

Ground floor with foyer.

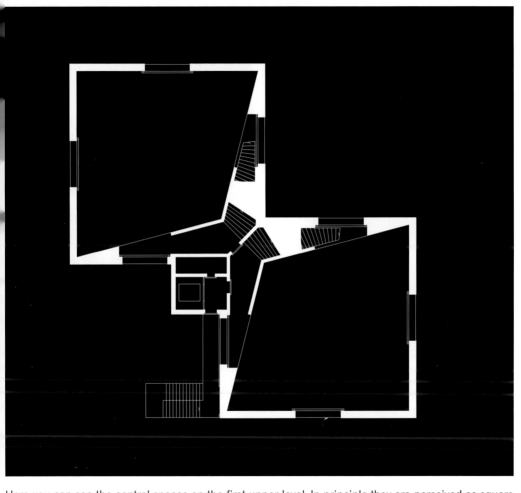

Here you can see the central spaces on the first upper level. In principle they are perceived as square rooms but with a slight distortion that lends the space a sense of movement. From each room you can look out to the north, south, east, and west.

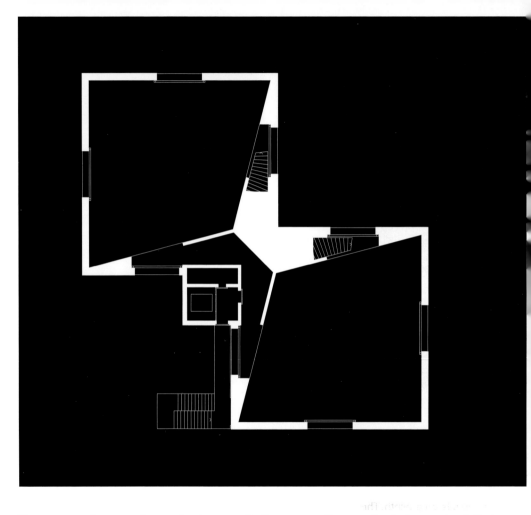

The rooms on the second upper level are exactly the same as those on the first upper level. Each room measures around 170–180 square meters, and the total floor space is around 400 square meters.

The building sits on a plinth. Three levels are visible. The window frames are set back and invisible so that you see only the concrete wall shell. The small jutties marking the transition to a new level indicate sections forming hollow bodies.

Everything is made of one material, an almost white concrete that has been poured without jointing. The floor has been sanded and then bush-hammered. The window frames and handrails are made of bronze.

The entrance is low. The sensation of walking through the wall is amplified by a lintel height of 1.9 meters. The visitor penetrates the wall to enter the interior, and another world. When standing in the middle of the rooms inside, the very deep window lintels lend the building a pronounced sense of introversion. However, the closer you stand to the window openings, or the edges of the rooms, the more the space begins to open up.

The floors consist of in-situ concrete sanded down to render the gravel, or the grain, visible. The external walls and the internal partition walls are made of insulating concrete.

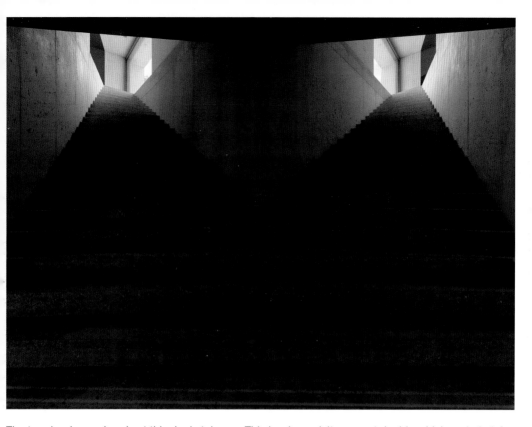

The tour begins and ends at this dual staircase. This is where visitors must decide which route to take, where they begin to reflect and attempt to comprehend the building in systematic terms, as it were. And it is at this point that they begin to see the building for what it is: simple from the outside but difficult to comprehend from the inside. This is the real true idea behind the building. Here we have a structure that is formed by two touching cubes with 25 identical windows that seems very simple and comprehensible. However, inside you are confronted by an almost labyrinthine world. Even after traversing the building and arriving outside again, after attempting to comprehend the building's internal interconnections, they still remain largely beyond your grasp.

The same room photographed twice in a diagonal perspective: once looking to the south and once to the north.

The same room photographed from opposite points.

Two views towards the east taken from different exhibition rooms on the same level. You can see in the upper photograph that the distance to the castle is somewhat shorter than in the lower photograph.

Staircase with connecting corridor.

Entrance to the exhibition room to the right at the end of the corridor.

The staircase is made of in-situ concrete, sanded and bush-hammered.

The building within the village.

The rear of the building showing the elevator, and fire escape. The fact that these two facilities do not form part of the building system precluded their being concealed in the interior. For this reason they have been consigned to the rear façade. It is only when you see the building from this perspective that it becomes clear that there are no hollow or double walls or floors—that no tricks are being played inside. This aspect is important for the expression of a labyrinthine character, since only genuine bewilderment can be convincing. And for me personally it is important that the actual idea remains pure—also in the mind.

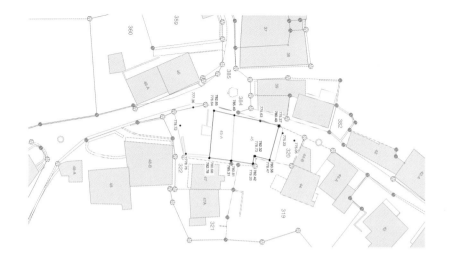

Now we come to the next project. The client is a well-known Swiss musician who lives with this family in Scharans, a small and very beautiful village. Around five years ago, he bought a barn there, which he wanted to have torn down and replaced with a new building. The site is part of the village core, a zone that is subject to a particularly large number of building regulations. Here in Scharans these regulations are virtually considered a matter of national interest. Over a period of three years we experimented with different project ideas. The client lives about fifty meters away in an old house with his family. For a long time it was unclear what he actually wanted to do with the building. Possibilities included a garden, a residential house, a studio with a small apartment, and so on. The client was personally in constant contact with the building authorities while we were developing the different project ideas. However, when we submitted our first project for approval, it was rejected on the basis that it would require too many planning exemptions. We then met with representatives from the municipality, who remained positively disposed towards our building design. A number of discussions with the mayor, the municipality's lawyer, and the municipal building consultant finally produced a new solution. This stipulated that the interest of the community in the character of its public space had to be respected. What this meant in practice was that the new building had to occupy exactly the same volume as the existing barn down to the last millimeter. Building would only be permitted on this condition. Our project thus had to conform to the shape of a barn built long ago by farmers, with all the random structural aspects that are included in such buildings. The yellow line shows where we could tear down the structure, and the red line shows where we were permitted to rebuild. As you can see these zones lie over one another.

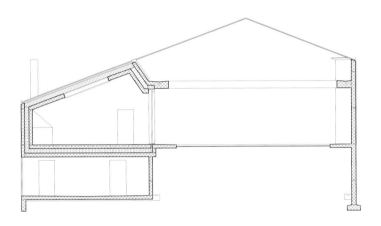

A cross section of the project. Here, the yellow line shows how the former silhouette of the barn was copied, a process in which particular attention had to be given to the gable.

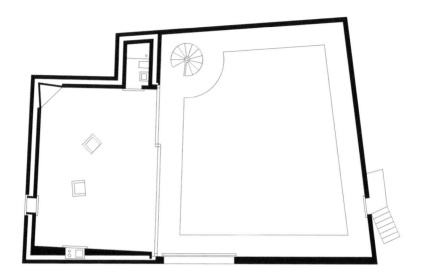

I would now like to explain the principle informing this building. The basic problem with all the legal requirements was that they ultimately stipulated a size that the client could not afford. The volume that was supposed to be built was simply too big and therefore too expensive. At first there did not seem to be a solution in sight. Then it occurred to me that an outside space that is not thermally insulated or heated could be constructed far more economically than a conditioned space. One of my staff then looked into the budgeting requirements for a conditioned and an unconditioned space. The result was that the dividing wall between the studio space and the courtyard needed to be positioned exactly where it is today, and where we can now see it in the ground plan. The relatively large courtyard space allowed us to keep within the budget. If the client had had more money, the courtyard would have been smaller. At the same time, and as luck would have it, the courtyard, measuring some 150 square meters, approximates a square within the ground plan. In relation to the surrounding village and its public streets and squares, these are monumental dimensions. These dimensions and this form made it possible to create a space with an absolutely controlled geometry within a structure conceived by farmers. It was actually at this point that I became enthusiastic about the project. Suddenly the random and organic was being confronted with the conceptual.

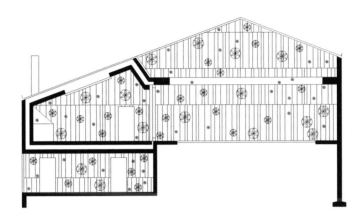

In this cross section we can see the only conditioned space within the building, and the studio, which measures 65 square meters. This is where the client writes and composes. After hearing the explanation for the budget, a friend of mine, a young lawyer, commented that his financial circumstances would probably have only allowed for a large courtyard with a heated toilet… We constructed a double-layered system out of concrete in which the interior space—floating, as it were, within the insulation is surrounded by an all-enclosing wall. The building is exclusively heated with solar panels, and is equipped with a heat-recovery ventilation system. The building is thus independent in terms of its energy requirements. Acoustic elements have been installed on the ceiling so that sound recordings can be made in the studio. The client also sometimes uses a mobile recording studio, which is parked in front of the building and connected to it by cables. The entire building is made of concrete. The round elements that can be seen in the plan are rosettes. Hundreds of these have been mounted on the interior and exterior walls as well as on the ceilings. I use concrete in almost all my projects. It is a material that enables me, as it were, to pour an idea in stone on the site itself. Pouring my structures lends them the character of an organism, the opposite of something modular.

The formwork is made of spruce from trees that are felled every spring in the forest around the village. A carpenter cut the wood into boards of different widths, allowed it to dry, and then planed it. Here you can see the storage area used for our formwork boards.

Here you can see how the rosettes are carved. When poured concrete is used, thought needs to be given to the appearance of the surface. We found the idea of tattooing a house very interesting. The ornaments are quotations stemming from the farming world. They have nothing to do with high culture or urban culture. The symbol is universal. I have not only seen this rosette in Europe, but also in Asia and South America. The naïve quality of the ornament reflects the rural cultural context of the building. However, rosettes of this type are otherwise found not on building façades, but on furniture. The fact that they are displayed here on the building has the effect of altering that building's character. The building becomes like a piece of furniture. A total of five hundred rosettes are found on the structure. We could use our formwork between three and five times. One hundred and fifty rosettes were carved by hand in two months by two cabinetmakers. Even the peripheral circles were drawn by hand without the use of a stencil. In-situ concrete has an extremely "artisanal" character, and there was no question of using a robot milling unit to make the rosettes. We decided on the manual method to avoid a break in the unitary expressiveness we were aspiring to.

A section of the concrete façade with concrete dyed in a red-brown color similar to terracotta red. At night the building appears brown, and in daylight more reddish. The appearance thus oscillates between earthiness and artificiality.

The façade contains a large opening into the interior courtyard measuring around three by three meters. The opening can be closed with a door, creating a haven with a single opening to the sky.

With opened door.

Some of the ornaments disappear into the ground but they actually begin at the level of the foundations. I am convinced that a building is understood in exactly the same way, as it is perceived. The notion that the ornaments are only where we can see them is intolerable and incomprehensible.

The view into the courtyard. In the pane of the sliding window to the left you can make out the reflection of the round roof opening.

Studio and courtyard. The sliding window is opened. It is operated with an electric motor since, at two and half tons, manual operation is out of the question. The window frame is larger than the opening in the concrete, and is concealed in the concrete rim so that it is invisible from the interior space. On the one hand, this creates a strong sense of openness. On the other hand, this construction is a response to the impossibility of keeping steel and concrete structures flush with one another. Exposed concrete has a degree of accuracy of at most one to two centimeters whereas steel has a degree of accuracy of one to two millimeters. It is therefore impossible to fit these two materials exactly together. The solution to this problem is usually the use of large, unsightly silicon joints. To avoid this in our building we have separated the concrete parts of our building with geometric clarity from structures made of more precise materials.

In the part of the courtyard shown here, you can see an apparently circular opening at the top, which is in reality elliptical. This cannot be discerned by the observer, who perceives the irregular, four-sided courtyard space as a square with a circular opening. This monumental aspect lends the space a sense of concept.

The open fireplace. Behind the door is a small toilet. Here, too, the concrete rim conceals the frames of the closed sliding windows. The glass is a specially manufactured clear glass that has no green or blue tones. Acoustic elements can be seen on the ceiling.

The open fireplace.

The left-hand outer wall becomes thicker towards the back in order to create a space for a small kitchen behind the doors to the left.

The entrance to the building.

In this picture you can see that the upper edges of the courtyard walls are covered with copper sheet. This provides the building with a roof, and the inner courtyard with shade. At the same time it creates an impression in the inner courtyard that it is surrounded by front façades, i.e. by buildings.

The project I want to show you now is a project for a competition we did not actually win. Nevertheless I want to show you this project because it allows me to make an important point about our approach to building a frame construction. For some years we have been experimenting with different aspects of frame construction. However, we have not yet had the opportunity to put these ideas into practice. As a result I am unable to show you a finished project here.

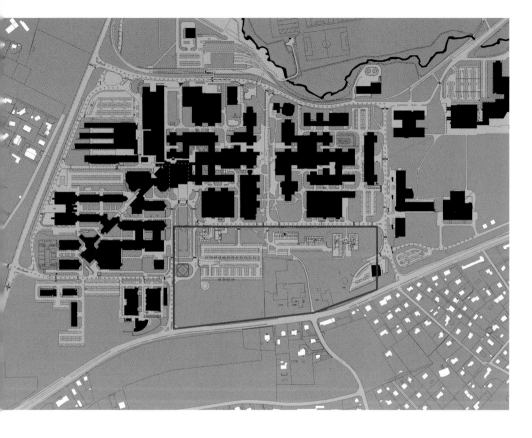

The design is for a new building for the EPFL Learning Center in Lausanne. Here you can see the site within the general plan of the campus at street level. The red line indicates the perimeter for the competition design, and the orange and blue lines the routes of public and private transport respectively. An unusual feature of this university is the fact that transport is found at ground level, but most pedestrian circulation is not.

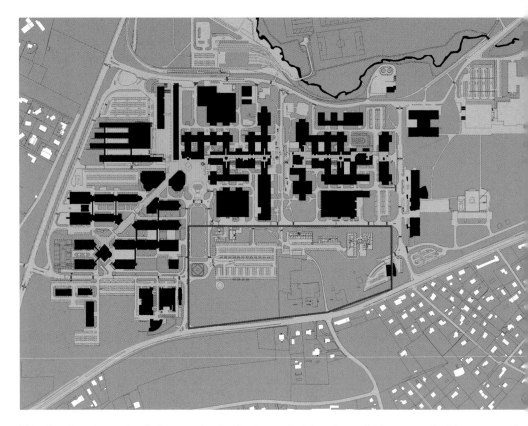

This drawing shows the first upper level with the route taken by pedestrians marked in orange. The pedestrian route runs along an axis that leads to the various faculties. Pedestrians need about eight minutes to walk from one end to the other. The task was to design a building for the area within the red perimeter in which facilities important for the whole campus could be located, including a library, a media center, offices, an auditorium, a restaurant, a café, a bookshop, and a language school. The idea was to create a place in which people from different faculties would meet and interact. The real question was, on the one hand, how to locate a center within a linear system and, on the other, how two systems on different levels could be linked with one another.

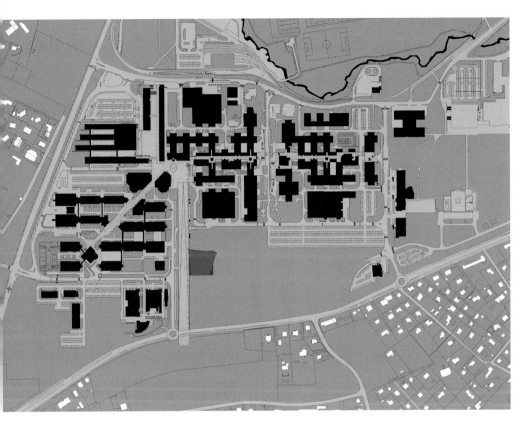

Our initial suggestion was to build to a thirty-meter wide ramp in order to link the pedestrian axis with the area defined by the competition perimeter. At the lower edge of the picture this ramp extends to the other side of the road, where the university is planning to build student apartments in the near future. The ramp would provide a direct connection for pedestrians with the central axis of the campus. We positioned the actual learning center building, marked here in red, next to this ramp.

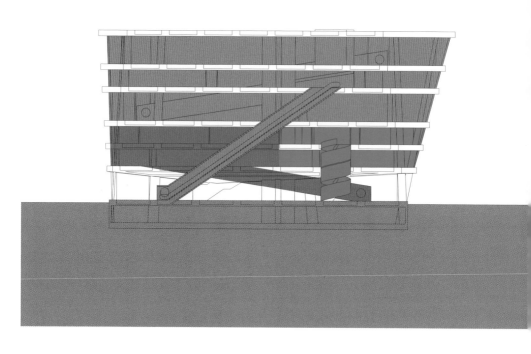

Here we see six different levels, with different colors used to indicate their functions. The ground level houses a completely open foyer without any dividing walls. From here you can access the upper levels. Each functional area is connected with the foyer on the ground level. The library and media center are accessed via an escalator, the restaurant via a spiral staircase, and the auditorium via a very wide ramp.

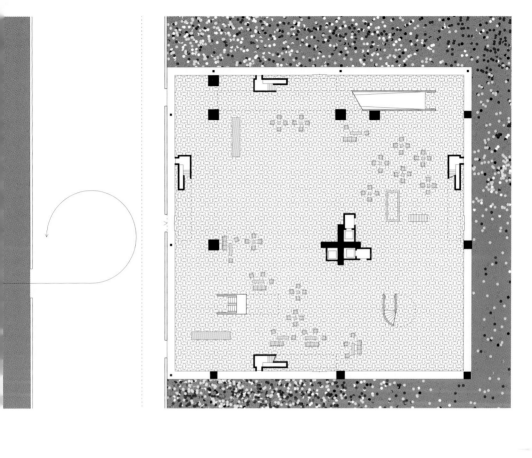

The floor plan of the ground level. All the walls are of glass and few structural elements are visible. The supporting structure is marked in black. The pillars measure 180 × 180 cm. At the outer rim you can see small posts, which measure 25 × 25 cm. As a whole, the structure initially appears to be uncoordinated.

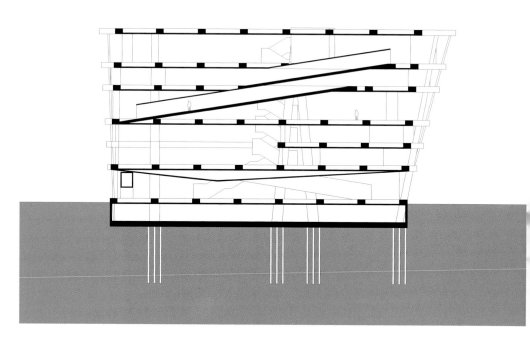

This cross section shows bracing ribs in the floors in which all the cables for the building can be housed.

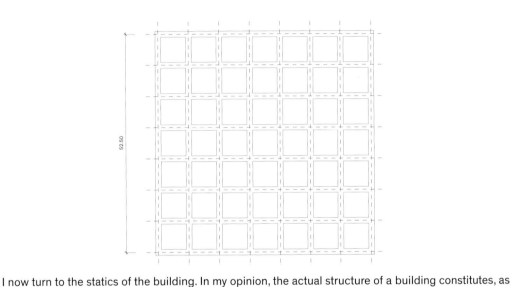

I now turn to the statics of the building. In my opinion, the actual structure of a building constitutes, as it were, the core focus of the logic applied by the architect, in so far as the architect is interested in logical thought. Personally, I find all other aspects of architecture arbitrary, and not rationally explicable. I often find myself in situations in which I cannot reach a decision. Architecture at the structural level, i.e. architecture that infringes on statics, requires the definition of criteria for decision making. When dealing with the science of statics, we find ourselves in the realm of the tangible. Furthermore, as I see it, the structural aspects of a building actually constitute the genetics of architecture, and for this reason require a good deal of thought. Dealing with the surface of a building is certainly also important, but architecture has been addressing this question constantly over the last thirty years and further contemplation is hardly going to revive architectural design. Here you can see the foyer located at ground level. It measures 52 × 52 meters. The ribs are 140 cm wide, and there are forty-nine fields with an axial dimension of 750 cm. This distance allows for conventional reinforcement of the concrete ceilings. This means that only the ribs, beams, and pillars require special reinforcement. The axes of the ribs are marked in blue.

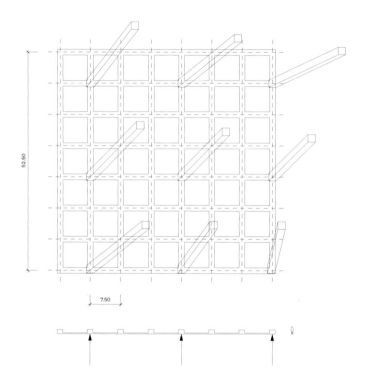

We decided to use nine pillars. The distance from pillar to pillar is 22.5 meters. These distances and the required overflow beams take us into the realm of bridge building. The problems associated with frame construction have less to do with vertical forces than with how horizontal forces resulting from wind or earthquakes are directed into the foundations.

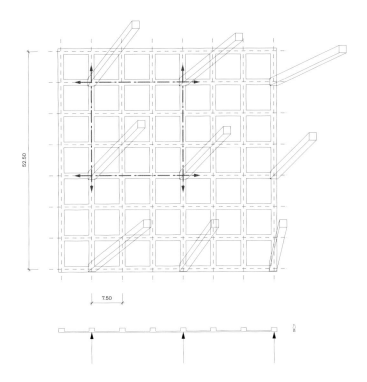

52.50

7.50

Stabilizing an area defined by four pillars against horizontal forces suffices here to reinforce the entire structure.

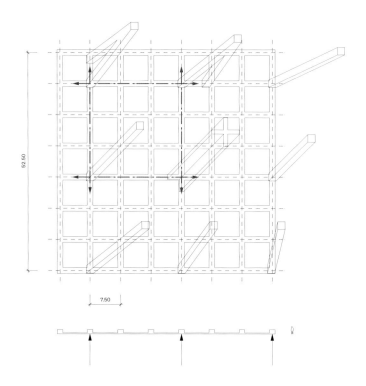

The cross-shaped pillar provides reinforcement in two directions, and the two A-form pillars stabilize the structure along the two other axes. The structure is thereby reinforced, and secured in all four directions.

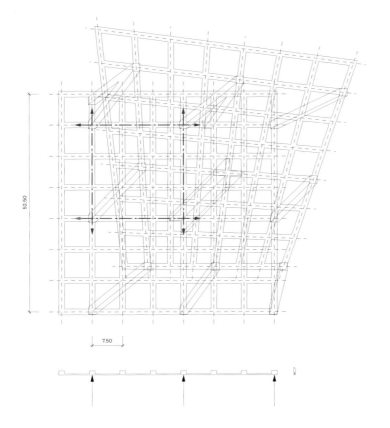

52.50

7.50

The intersection points of the rib axes each lie on the midpoint of a pillar. We then decided that all the floor plates should be exactly the same size. This means that each floor covers exactly the same number of square meters. These two parameters lead to an increasing distortion of the floor plates as the building rises, such that the original square becomes trapezoid. The result is that at the level you enter the building, the space that constitutes the central focus of the campus is constructed as a square. And as the building rises this square becomes distorted, as it were, arbitrarily.

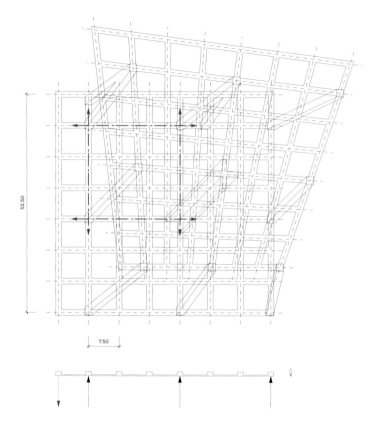

52.50

7.50

Now we come to the cantilever. Here we can make the entire structure even more efficient, and somewhat slimmer. Imagine that if we sit on a table it will then bend in the middle and the ends will rise. The same applies to our structure. In order to avoid this effect, we have attached load cables to the rib structure, therefore the ends are pulled downwards. This is indicated here by the red arrow. Reinforced concrete consists of a mixture of, on the one hand, gravel and cement and, on the other hand, of steel. The gravel and cement mixture is subject to pressure, the steel to tension. In the case of our structure this means we have to concrete our load cables in the form of a pillar measuring 25×25 cm.

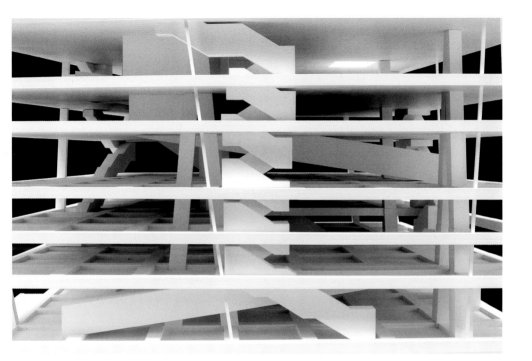

Here you can see the model of the structural framework. Although everything accords with a specific logic, the first impression is chaotic and emotional. The structure appears incomprehensible. However, once you have comprehended the basic form, everything else appears completely logical. This is a construction with an absolutely logical basis. If we removed one beam or pillar, the building would not only partially but also completely collapse in the next earthquake. This is not a frame construction that functions like a conventional pillar-plate system, in which elements are placed next to and stacked on one another. It is not a modular system, where elements are organized adjacent to and on top of one another. This structure is different. It is comparable with a plant; it has an organic character. Everything is dependent on everything else; every part grows out of another, and into the next one. All of this is only possible with reinforced concrete. This network of interdependencies cannot be developed with metal, wood, or brick, but only with reinforced concrete. Only reinforced concrete allows me to develop what is, so to speak, a genuine organism.

The spiral staircase into the restaurant.

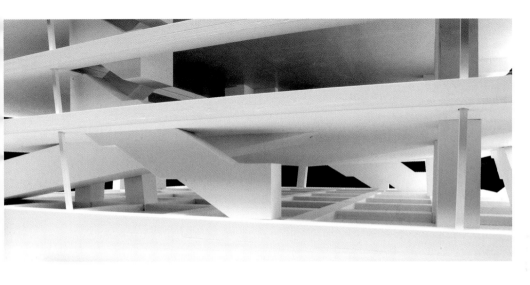

The fire escape staircase, and behind it the ramp into the auditorium, packed into a rectangular pipe.

Here the A-pillars are clearly visible.

Now a number of renderings.

Here you can clearly see the dimensions. A person standing in the picture provides an idea of the dimensions involved.

The entrance into the building.

The foyer with its square floor plan. As you can see, the ceiling forms an inverted pyramid. The lowest point, the actual peak, is located exactly above the diagonal intersection of the floor plate. The ceiling is thus low in the middle of the space, and becomes gradually higher towards the windows. As a result the space opens up towards the outside, and when you walk through the room, the different heights are perceived as a moving mass. On the other hand, this impression provides the foyer with a protective atmosphere.

The building from the outside.

Here you can see a photo of the exhibition of my work held at the Swiss Federal Institute of Technology (ETH) in Zurich. White models, on a scale of 1:33, together with plans and photographs of the buildings. I would like to talk about the depictions on the plates sitting just above the floor. These feature pictures that are not directly connected with the exhibited projects.

Some time ago I decided to attempt to explain my architecture in the form of pictures rather than words—using a total of 55 images. This involves a highly associative form of explanation. The pictures present things that I find very interesting, either in terms of motif, composition, or content. It would have been possible to select a thousand pictures, but in the process of reflection and selection the number became smaller and smaller. In the end it was precisely these images that remained. These are images that influence me, and that come to mind when I think about my architecture. I call this personal collection an "iconographic autobiography."

The first picture is of a small etching from the nineteenth century showing Lake Como. I should first give you some background information here. My father, who was also an architect, and who influenced my own work, hung this picture in a frame next to my bed at head height soon after I was born. You have to imagine that during my childhood this picture hung some forty centimeters from my head. I grew up with this picture. Every morning when I woke up it was the first thing I saw. My father manipulated me with this picture in the sense that it programmed me with his own bias in matters of taste, and I find myself still carrying this influence with me today. Whenever I am faced with a decision, my starting point is the kind of classical situation depicted in this etching. If I could, I would construct buildings like the one in this picture. I also like this wonderful boat floating alone on the surface of the water, steered by a lone figure.

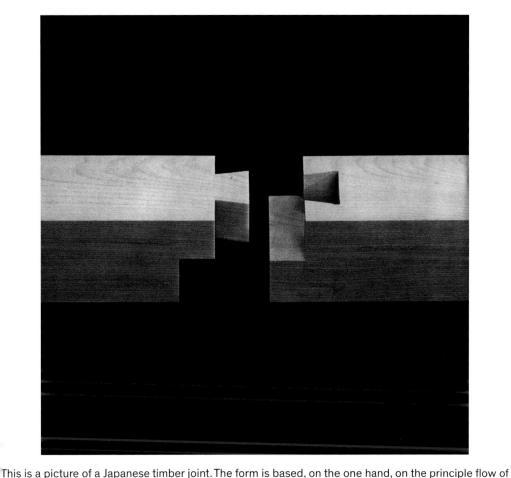

This is a picture of a Japanese timber joint. The form is based, on the one hand, on the principle flow of force in a three-dimensional form and, on the other, on the specific properties of wood. The result is a highly precise example of manual work. When it comes to architecture, in my opinion a precise concept demands precise implementation. I do not think, for example, that poor financial circumstances can be used to explain or even justify poor quality implementation.

This is a photo taken in Machu Picchu in Peru. It shows the sidewall of an Inca temple. The very large pieces of granite used here have been shaped and fitted together with an almost unbelievable precision. I would argue that the question of precision among the Incas should not be interpreted solely in terms of technique. I believe that the Incas attempted to create a sacred building in a form that defied earthly assumptions and possibilities. For example, the stones were shaped and fitted together over a period of ninety years and several generations. The precision shown here is the expression of an absolute understanding.

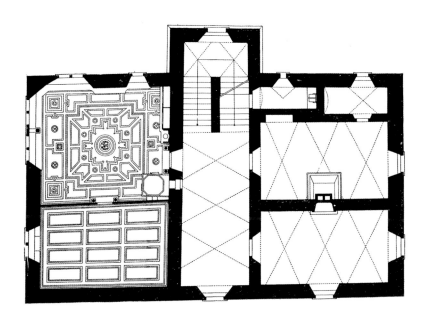

This is the floor plan of a patrician house from around 1650. It comes from the canton of Grisons, where I come from, and where I live today. The house is very clearly constructed: to the right of the corridor there are rooms featuring stone, plasterwork, and vaulted ceilings. To the left are richly decorated rooms lined with wood. This duality is one of the principles underlying the traditional architecture of Grisons. It does not involve the attempt to achieve a nuanced relationship, a harmonized reconciliation of two different characters, but rather a fairly demonstrative determination to live in two fundamentally different worlds directly adjacent to one another. This approach corresponds very precisely to the character of Grisons culture.

The Taj Mahal. For me it represents one of the great architectural experiences, perhaps the greatest, and verges on a revelation. Surrounded by endlessly beautiful buildings made of earth-colored, red-brown stone, the Taj Mahal is made completely of the kind of glowing white marble that you associate with an epiphany. A pure idea.

This is an Indo-Persian miniature that I myself own. It is not much bigger than a postcard. The house is located exactly in the middle of the garden. Four paths lead to it from the four cardinal points of the compass. The garden is surrounded by a wall, and the entrance is located at the end of one of the paths. Three women are in the house, at the center of the world. The wall is earth-colored, and the house is white. The house symbolizes paradise, and the wall symbolizes the world. In my view, the color white represents the imagination, and red-brown represents reality.

Monte Albàn in Mexico. The pre-Columbian complex is located on top of a mountain in the valley of Oaxaca. The valley is around fifty kilometers wide and many times that in length. Some two thousand years ago Zapotecs removed the peak of the mountain to create a platform. The mountain stands like the stump of a pyramid in the valley. The earthen floor of the platform was originally paved as smoothly as smooth as a mirror. Temples and pyramids stood here. It is not known what the functions of the individual buildings were, or the principle according to which they were arranged on the platform. However, we do know that the Zapotecs very precisely studied the cosmos, and that they constructed their interpretation of the universe here on this platform. You need to imagine moving across the Oaxaca valley towards this mountain, climbing it, and then arriving amidst the pyramids on this absolutely horizontal platform. You find yourself between sky and platform, surrounded by objects that mirror the cosmos. You now begin to feel as if you were perched on a mighty object travelling through the universe—an unbelievable sensation of a space of gigantic dimensions.

Fatehpur Sikri in India, built by the Mogul Akbar in the second half of the sixteenth century. Everything, absolutely everything, you can see in this picture is built of a single material, stone—very hard stone. The building represents a fusion of two opposites in a single material, the monotheistic culture of Islam, and the polytheistic culture of Hinduism, a fusion that is both abstract and representative. Fatehpur Sikri is the most beautiful object that I have ever seen. It embodies everything that I would describe as beautiful or passionate.

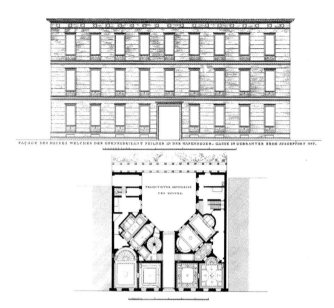

FAÇADE DES HAUSES WELCHES DER OFENFABRIKANT FEILNER IN DER HASENHEGER- GASSE IN GEBRANTER ERDE AUSGEFÜHRT HAT.

A building in Berlin by Karl Friedrich Schinkel that unfortunately no longer exists. The façade is regular and symmetrically constructed. It communicates to us immediately that the building is clearly structured and absolutely comprehensible. But this initial impression is also completely deceptive. This is a building with a highly complex, almost labyrinthine design. The plan itself bears a very complicated description: "FAÇADE OF THE HOUSE BUILT BY THE OVEN MANUFACTURER HASENHEGER GASSE IN BAKED EARTH." Quite a story! We can now go into the room directly to the right of the entrance. We enter the building via a corridor, turn left, climb a stairway, and then turn right into a room with a round apse and a window to the courtyard. Once inside this room, we turn ninety degrees, and walk through a connecting passage into another room, in this case directly through an apse. This room has two windows looking onto the street. Now we finally enter the room mentioned at the outset through yet another door positioned on the axis of symmetry. Here at the very latest we become completely disorientated. We have no points of reference anymore that we can relate to the order within which we normally negotiate an architectural structure.

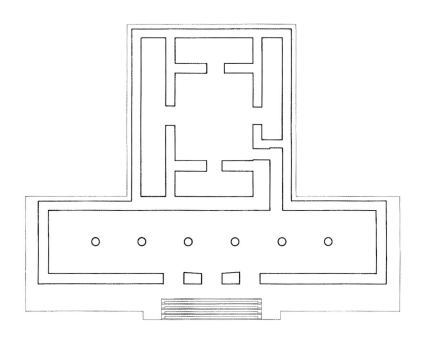

Here you can see a diagram of Mitla, the floor plan of a pre-Columbian temple around two thousand years old. Of particular interest here are the two main rooms, the elongated one at the bottom and the quadratic one at the top. Although the elongated room is equipped with columns, the quadratic room is the more important one since it constitutes the central space. It is also located deeper in the temple's interior. It is the actual destination rather than a room that is passed through. The passage that links the two rooms is outside the main ordering axes, and is divided into two loosely touching spatial zones. It is subordinate to the system as a whole. In this architecture it is neither the symbolism nor the motifs that create the underlying meaning, but rather the geometry, and the position of the rooms.

The Palazzo Dei Priori in Volterra. The ledge around the bottom of the building creates the impression that the structure is floating just above the ground. The building stands in the city like a piece of furniture; it is a total object and very beautiful. It represents the antithesis of the contemporary concept of an objectless city, a dreadful notion devised by incapable architects who propagate the idea of architecture without authors.

Santa Catalina in Peru, a women's cloister in Arequipa. This city was founded by Spaniards in the sixteenth century in the Peruvian desert. The entire cloister complex constitutes a city quarter several hundred meters in length and breadth. The right-angled streets lead through the cloister as they do through other quarters of the city. You enter the cloister almost without realizing it; it is only the large, closable gates on the arterial streets that mark the point of transition. The colors used are interesting: red-brown and blue. Red-brown marks the public street spaces and blue the private areas reserved for the nuns. The nuns' rooms are dematerialized, and the streets outside are earthbound. It is a stark opposition based on careful reflection—a precise idea driven by a fundamental intent.

The dining table in our kitchen in Flims. My wife and I are very fond of Italian food, certainly more so than we are of French cuisine. When you have Italian food in your mouth you experience a single taste unlike French food, which always involves many different flavors, a mixture—perhaps successful or unsuccessful—of innumerable things. In my opinion it is vital that an architect should know what food suits his or her taste.

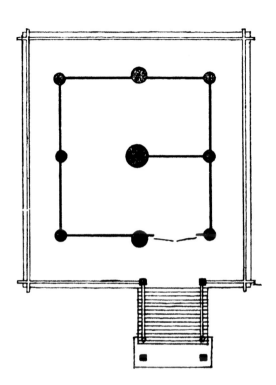

A floor plan of the Izumo-taisha shrine in Japan, which is made of wood. You can see nine columns, all of which are stripped tree trunks. In the middle of the quadratic inner room you can see the thickest of these columns, the broadest trunk. This holds the building, as it were, in position, even in a strong cross wind—like the trunk of a tree that simultaneously supports the crown and prevents the tree from tipping over. You enter the room asymmetrically and see a wall that touches the central column, thereby divesting the interior room of a center. Without this wall the room would be dominated by a column that would thus for no obvious reason be celebrated. This simple wall prevents such an incorrect reading of the space.

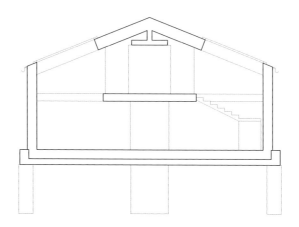

Now I come to the last project, our office that we built in Flims two years ago. As with the building in Scharans, this site was occupied by a barn that had to be torn down, and replaced by a new building that more or less mirrored the external form of the old building. This meant that the form, the subdivisions, and the dimensions had to be based on a preexisting model. The cross section here shows the building set on pillars with two upper floors that house the actual office. Each floor measures around 110 square meters. This means that we do not have a very large office and that we have to limit the number of people working there. This was a conscious decision. You can also see large windows in the roof that let light into the interior of the space. The lower part—the table with legs, so to speak—is made of concrete while the upper, conditioned part is made of wood. Building regulations in the municipality of Flims specify that either wood or plaster must be used, and we decided on wood.

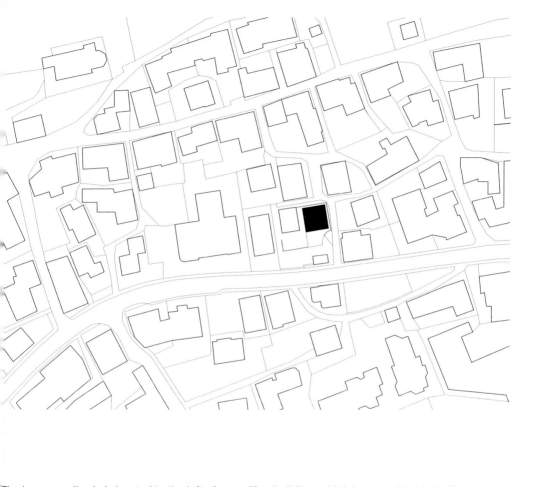

The house we live in is located to the left of new office building, which is marked in black. The house is around two hundred and fifty years old, and my father, who was, as I have already mentioned, also an architect, constantly remodelled it throughout his life. We have lived in this house since my father's death—for many years only on weekends, and now permanently.

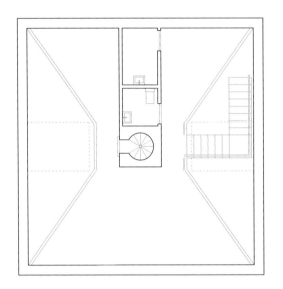

I would now like to explain the floor plan to you, and will begin with the loft at the top. This houses the meeting room, as well as a small kitchenette, and a toilet. To the right and left of the core there are large openings, which have been vertically glazed for acoustic reasons, and from where you can see into the lower level. These also allow daylight to penetrate to the lower level from the large roof window.

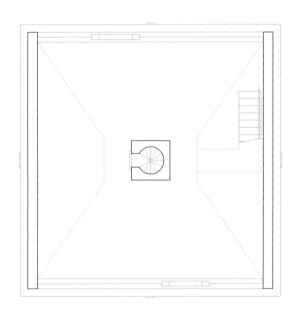

This is the main level, and it is here that we work. Depending on the how we've organized the tables, between 12 and 16 people work here. The main entrance to the building can be seen at the top of the floor plan. To the right you can see a staircase that leads to the meeting room in the loft. This means that all areas of our office are easily accessible. In the middle you can see a very narrow spiral staircase, which is used by my wife and I. This is where our private realm begins, so to speak. This staircase links the office spaces with the covered space adjoining the garden, and the private parking spaces. We reach our house through the garden. This means that we can enter or leave all levels whenever we like. The core of the staircase is made of concrete, and apart from the outside staircase, it is the only concrete part of the building that is otherwise constructed from timber.

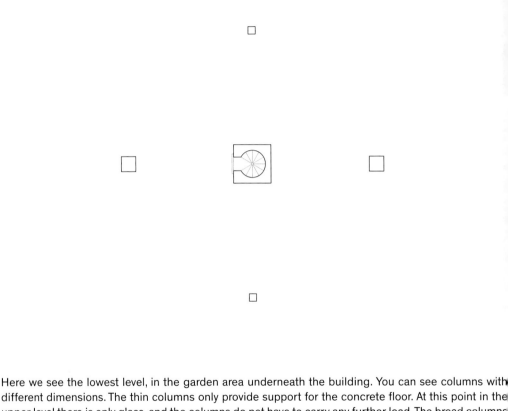

Here we see the lowest level, in the garden area underneath the building. You can see columns with
different dimensions. The thin columns only provide support for the concrete floor. At this point in the
upper level there is only glass, and the columns do not have to carry any further load. The broad columns
to the right and left support not only the concrete floor, but also the walls of the wooden structure. It is
via these columns that the load from the wooden building and snow on the roof is directed into the
foundations. You can also see the continuous concrete core in the middle, which, on the one hand
absorbs the vertical load of the building and, on the other, reacts to the horizontal forces caused by
wind or earthquakes. This core forms, as it were, the trunk that prevents the entire tree from tipping over

The view of the building from the main road. The wooden construction is made of normal spruce that we have colored black. To the left, somewhat hidden, you can see our white house.

There are no corner posts that we usually find in more conventional structures. The covered space adjoining the garden is a genuine outside space without any conventional spatial emphasis on the corners. In the background, you can see our house. It stands in the midst of the lawn, and is white—my father only built white houses throughout his life. The office, which is black, stands on asphalt. We live in the white building and work in the black one. In my opinion white spaces have an introverted character and black have an extroverted one. The line between asphalt and lawn is located precisely on the central axis of the site. This is where the two "carpets" intersect on which our two buildings are constructed.

The concrete wall in the background supports the surrounding slope. The building and the wall do not touch one another; there is an open space between them around 30 centimeters wide. Asphalt is the material of the streets, the public space. As soon as the garage gate is opened, the covered garden becomes part of the street—or more importantly, the street becomes part of the garden. The opening and closing of the gate significantly alters the character of the garden.

A view towards the uphill wall. The surface of the concrete is very conventional and is acquiring a patina as time passes.

Here you can see the dimensions of the cantilever, which were achieved using pre-stressed concrete.

The view from the rear. The building appears to stand on a heavy plinth. The main entrance to the office can be seen in the right-hand field of the glazing.

The interior space. Here, too, everything is made of black-colored wood. The reason for this use of black, as already mentioned, is based on my perception of very dark space as extroverted and thus public. This is just the opposite in the case of a white space. In the past we traveled intensively in America and visited over fifty buildings built by Frank Lloyd Wright. Particularly in the old buildings, the windows are very small in relation to the façade surface and the materials in the interior are often very dark. Nevertheless, all these spaces exhibit a very pronounced reference to the outside. The surrounding landscape positively glows, the presence of the external space is extremely strong and the dark interior walls are not reflected in the windows when you are looking out into the external space. The dark spaces recede into the background and are dominated by the surroundings. By contrast, the open, snow-white spatial structures by Richard Meier seem extremely closed. The interior spaces are illuminated and self-referential, and the white walls are reflected in the glass windows when you are looking out into the external exterior space. The glass walls become an enclosing membrane. It is for this reason that we decided to design a black building. The space inside our building is low and, combined with the horizontal format of the windows, becomes an observation space corresponding to the way we human beings see things through two horizontally positioned eyes. In contrast to the black receding into the background, the worktables are all made of white plastic.

Here you can see how the light from the rooflight radiates into the interior of the space.

Another contrast between interior and exterior. To the right you can see the stairs leading to the loft level.

The meeting room in the loft. This is where we sit and devise our projects.

We developed the method of coloring the wood with a materials technologist. The coloring consists of three layers: water, spirit, and linseed oil, all supplemented with black pigment. Linseed oil was used for the final layer in order to create a light gloss.

The main level. To the right you can see the reflection in the glazing on the loft level.

The final picture. This is the table occupied by the project manager who built our office—illuminated, so to speak, from above.

Imprint   Olgiati   A Lecture by Valerio Olgiati   The lecture was held in German and translated into the
other relevant languages. Concept: Valerio Olgiati; graphic design: Dino Simonett and Bruno Margreth;
project coordination: Andrea Wiegelmann; translation Joe O'Donnell; editing: Markus Breitschmid,
Leina Gonzales;   bibliographical information listed in the German National Library; the German National
Library has registered this publication in the Deutsche Nationalbibliografie; detailed bibliographical
data is available online at http://dnb.d-nb.de. © 2011 Birkhäuser GmbH, Basel; Postfach, 4002 Basel,
Switzerland; an ActarBirkhäuser company   Printed in Germany   ISBN 978-3-0346-0783-4   This
work is also published in German ISBN 978-3-0346-0782-7, French ISBN 978-3-0346-0784-1, Italian
ISBN 978-3-0346-0785-8, Spanish ISBN 978-3-0346-0787-2 and Japanese ISBN 978-3-0346-
0786-5   9 8 7 6 5 4 3 2 1   www.birkhauser.com